George White

A Brief Account of the Life, Experience, Travels, and Gospel Labours of George White, an African; Written by Himself, and Revised by a Friend

George White

b. 1764

LARGE PRINT EDITION

George White

A BRIEF ACCOUNT
OF THE LIFE, EXPERIENCE, TRAVELS,
AND GOSPEL LABOURS OF GEORGE
WHITE, AN AFRICAN;
WRITTEN BY HIMSELF,
AND REVISED BY A FRIEND.
By
George White

God hath chosen the foolish things of the world to confound the wise: and base things of the world, and things that are despised, hath God chosen, yea, and things that are not, to bring to nought things that are: that no flesh should glory in his presence.

ST. PAUL.

NEW YORK:
PRINTED BY JOHN C. TOTTEN,
No. 155 Chatham-street.
1810.

George White

A Brief Account

PREPARED FOR PUBLICATION

BY

HISTORIC PUBLISHING

TO THE READER.

As reading the account of the lives, and religious experience of others, has often quickened and comforted my own soul, and encouraged me in the way to heaven, I feel it my duty to present the friends of Jesus with a short detail of the dealings of God towards me; in my conversion, temptations, religious conflicts, call to preach, and sufferings therein; hoping to administer some of those benefits to them, which I have derived from the writings of others on the same subject: to which I have subjoined with the same view, an account of the extraordinary death of two persons of my own acquaintance, the one very pious, and the other very wicked: as also some remarks on the subject of true happiness.

When I consider the station in which I am placed, and the obligations I am under, especially to my African brethren, I rejoice at every opportunity of facilitating their spiritual welfare and happiness. And should the present undertaking prove conducive thereto, the reader will do me the pleasure, to ascribe the honor and glory to God; while he enjoys the proposed benefit.

And that, whoever reads the following relation, may be blessed of God, and eternally saved in Jesus Christ, is the most affectionate and fervent prayer of their sincere friend and brother, in the kingdom and patience of Christ Jesus,

GEORGE WHITE.

New York, April 10, 1810.

BRIEF ACCOUNT, &C.

MY mother was a slave, belonging to an estate in the township of Accomack, state of Virginia, where I was born in the fall of 1764: but at the age of one year and a half, was torn from her fond embraces, and carried by my owner into Esther county; where I was kept until six years of age; being treated with a degree of indulgence, uncommon to the children of Virginian slaves. However, about this time, my master, for reasons best known to himself, sold me to a person in Sommerset county, state of Maryland; from whom I received much better treatment than is usual for Africans to meet with, in this land of human oppression and barbarity. Here I continued in servitude, until the fifteenth year of my age; when I was again made merchandize of, sold, and sent into Suffolk; where I continued under all the severities of the most abject slavery, till I arrived at the twenty-sixth year of my age.

When about nineteen, the sympathy of nature, awakened in my mind, such a sense of filial affection, that the thoughts of my enslaved, but loving parents, deprived me of my necessary rest; and my frequent inquiries about, and carnest entreaties to visit them, though very offensive to my master, yet at length prevailed with him, to give me permission to return to the place of my nativity, to see my mother, who, as I was informed by one of her acquaintance, was yet living.   As my mother knew not what had become of me, the reader will easily imagine the affecting nature and circumstances of the scene of the first meeting, of a parent lost, and a child unknown; and both in a state of the most cruel bondage, without the means, or even hope of relief. But our joyful interview of mingling anguish, was of but short duration; for my condition, as a slave, would not admit of my prolonging the visit beyond the day appointed for my return: therefore we were obliged to undergo the painful sensations, occasioned by a second parting; and I, to return to my former servitude, in despair of ever obtaining an emancipation.

However, the infinitely wise disposer of all events, called my master to the world of spirits, when I was about twenty-six: and so far humanized his heart, that he left me free at his death; although it was with great difficulty, that I saved myself from the renewal of my thralldom, which was attempted by the heirs to his estate.

Perhaps nothing can be more conducive to vice and immorality, than a state of abject slavery, like that practiced by the Virginia planters upon the degraded Africans: For being deprived by their inhuman masters and overseers, of almost every privilege and enjoyment, in their absence, without much restraint or reserve, fall into those practices, which are contrary to the well-being of society, and repugnant to the will of God, whenever opportunity offers.

But after I had obtained my freedom, (a blessing quite unexpected) I began to think, that, as God in his providence had delivered me from temporal bondage, it was my duty to look to him for deliverance from the slavery of sin; that I might be prepared to make him suitable returns for so great a favor.

I had often attended public worship in the Church of England, but without any sufficient evidence of being benefited thereby. The Methodists happening about this time, to hold a quarterly meeting in Annimissick I repaired thither; and was considerably alarmed with a sense of my sins, and enabled to form resolutions for life, very different from those I had before.

Having now, no other master but him, whose protecting care had brought me to the present period, and had inspired my mind with a desire to seek his face, I felt anxious to become more acquainted with Christian people; and hearing that the Africans were treated with less severity and contempt in the northern, than in the southern states, I resolved to evade these scenes of brutal barbarity, which I had so long witnessed in my native land, and so set off for the city of New-York: which place, however, I did not reach till about three years after; finding good employ in the interim, at Philadelphia, and in the state of New-Jersey, which induced me to tarry at those places.

In the year 1791, it pleased my Almighty preserver, in his good providence, to bring me in safety to this place, where I resided several years before I set out with my whole heart to seek a saving interest in Jesus Christ; yet was not without the strivings of the Divine Spirit. But under the preaching of the Rev. Mr.

Stebbens, from, "The axe is laid unto the root of the trees," (on a memorable watch-night, held in the Bowery Church) I experienced such a manifestation of the Divine power, as I had before been a stranger to: and under a sense of my amazing sinfulness in the sight of God, I fell prostrate on the floor, as one wounded or slain in battle; and indeed I was slain by the law, that I might be made alive by Jesus Christ.

The distress of my mind at this time, was such as no language can describe, and can only be apprehended by those who have labored under the same weight and burden of sin, conscious of their own just condemnation, as rebels against the righteous government of God. However, I soon found a degree of encouragement and relief to my sin-sick soul, though not the clear evidence of my acceptance in the beloved. Soon after this, I joined the Methodist society.

The followers of the despised Jesus now became more than ever the excellent of the earth in my view, and in their society, I took great delight. But the enemy of my soul, by whom I had so long been enslaved, unwilling to lose his prey, beset me on every side, and brought me into a new scene of distress. Had not the Lord sustained my feeble mind under the sore conflicts I endured, I must have fallen a victim to the rage of the infernal foe.

But thanks be to God, his grace was sufficient for me; and I may truly say, his strength was made perfect in my weakness; and by the light of his Spirit, shining upon my disconsolate soul, he cheered my heart with his love, and revived my languid hope, which encouraged me to persevere in the way of righteousness.

In the year 1804, I attended a Camp Meeting, being one of the first held in this district. A large concourse of people, of all descriptions, convened on the occasion, of which, many were made the subjects of saving grace, and believers were filled with perfect love. At this meeting, the Lord, in a more powerful manner than ever, made known his salvation to me, by the influences and witness of his Holy Spirit; so that, when the exercises were over, I left the hallowed place with a glow of heavenly joy, which none but God himself can inspire.

Sometime after this, I had the following most affecting, interesting, and frightful dream, or night vision. After the usual religious exercises in my family, I retired to rest at the late hour of about two in the morning; and falling to sleep, the place of the future torment of the wicked was presented to my view, with all its dreadful horrors. It was a pit, the depth and extent of which were too vast for my discovery; but perfectly answering the description given of it in holy writ--a lake burning with fire and brimstone; which has enlarged her mouth without measure, and is moved from beneath, to meet the wicked at their coming.

The descent into this place of misery, was by a series of steps, the top of which was near the surface of the earth. In it, I saw vast multitudes of souls, suffering the torments of the damned; out of whose mouths and nostrils issued flames of fire; and from these flames an impenetrable cloud of smoke continually ascended; and being attended by a guide, he bade me take particular notice of what was passing, in, and about this hedious gulph; upon which I be-held an host of evil spirits, continually employed in leading human souls to the place of descent into this bottomless pit; at which they were received by other devils, who awaited their coming, and dragged them headlong down the steps, to meet their final doom.

But one, which I particularly observed, and doubted from its smallness and singular appearance, whether it was a human being, had no sooner arrived at this place of misery, than it assumed the features and size of a man, and began, with all the other newcomers, to emit flames of fire, from the mouth and nostrils, like those I had seen there at first.

I next beheld a coach, with horses richly furnitured, and full of gay, modish passengers, posting to this place of torment; but, when they approached the margin of the burning lake, struck with terror and dismay, their countenances changed, and awfully bespoke their surprise and fear.

But having myself, while engaged with my conductor, stepped upon the top of the descent, and apparently burnt my feet, which he observing, said to me, "Go, and declare what you have seen." Upon which I awoke; but so overcome by the effect of what I had seen, that it was a considerable time before I was able to speak.

Having recovered a little from the anguish of my mind, occasioned by this distressing scene, I related the whole to my bosom companion; who, having heard it with astonishment, and much affection, was desirous to know what I thought would be the result; concerning which, I gave her my opinion in full; and we covenanted together from that time, to be more faithful to God than ever, and to escape, if possible, the torments I had seen.

From a belief, that it was my duty to call sinners to repentance, I communicated my exercises on the subject, to my Christian brethren:--But a person of long experience in the way of godliness, from whom I expected encouragement, said, If you are going to preach, I will quit.

However, I thought with myself, that the best and safest method I could pursue, was, to yield obedience to the command of him, who I believed had called me to this duty; trusting alone in his promises, providence, and grace. Accordingly I applied for a trial hearing, in order to obtain license as an exhorter; to which the brethren consented, and I made my first attempt to speak in public in the month of April, 1805; but with much fear and trembling; being sensible of my inability and ignorance: for at this time I had not so much learning, as even the knowledge of the English alphabet; but in my broken way could talk of Christ, and his love to sinners, which I did according to the best of my abilities. But the brethren, after hearing what I had to say, concluded that it would be improper to give me license, which brought fresh trials upon my mind: yet I endeavored to keep what the Lord had committed to me

From a conviction that God had called me to labor in public, and the distressing fear, lest the enemy of souls should take an advantage of my neglect, and entirely rob me of my confidence, and undo me forever, I passed away several months in a most gloomy and distressing state of mind, deprived, both of slumber and appetite.

My only consolation, during this season of trials, was derived from reflecting upon the greatness, goodness, and power of God; as being adequate to the accomplishment of whatever seemeth him good; which encouraged me to place my whole dependence upon him; in hope that he would clear my way before me: for he still seemed to say, "Go--warn the wicked to flee from the wrath to come."

Under these exercises, in the month of July, I solicited the brethren to give me a second hearing; with which they complied, and the Lord gave us a powerful and happy season, while waiting upon him; by enabling me to speak, and blessing his word to them that heard. After consulting on the subject, the brethren agreed that I should have license to exhort; which was matter of no small joy to my soul, being thereby relieved from my former embarrassment, and at liberty to do the will of God, without transgressing the order of his church.

The importance of the work assigned me now, engrossed all my thoughts, and I resolved to improve what ability the Lord had given me, to exhort all, both men and women, to repent and turn to that God who had set my own soul at liberty.

Having a desire to travel. I left New-York and proceeded to Long-Island, where I went from village to village, exhorting the people to seek the Lord, for I soon found there was but little religion among them, which, though it gave me much sorrow, engaged me the more in urging them to seek it, not only by argument, but by giving them a narrative of my own experience, in the love of God.

But to do justice to the inhabitants of this island, even those who appear to be destitute of religion, are, nevertheless, generous and kind.

Having now fixed the limits of my rout, I continued my exhortations among them. While in this exercise, at a place called New-Lots, the word so reached the heart of a woman in the congregation, that she cried aloud for mercy, and though opposed and ridiculed by some professed deists who were present, she professed to find peace with God.

Travelling to the eastward, I stopped at Babylon, where a meeting had been appointed for me, at the house of Mr. Conklin. This gentleman is not only hospitable, but a friend to religion. My congregation here consisted of about fifty persons, among whom a deep solemnity reigned during the exercises; and numbers of them, I have no doubt, are now happy in the Savior, having caught the holy fire at that meeting; which was astonishingly manifested at the time.

During this tour upon the island, I saw more of the manifestations of the power and love of God, and the different means, by which he effects the work of grace in the souls of men, than I had known before.

Many who knew not Christ, were awakened and converted, in a most extraordinary manner, being smitten to the earth by the power of God; which, with a number of other circumstances, led me more fully than ever, to reflect upon the importance of the work, I had undertaken for Christ's sake; which exercised my own mind to that degree, under a sense of the necessity of a clean heart, that I could not rest till God should sanctify my soul, and thereby, the better prepare me for his service.

Under these exercises, I returned to the city of New-York, and in the month of May, 1806, at a meeting held in my own house. I fell prostrate upon the floor, like one dead. But while I lay in this condition, my mind was vigorous and active; and an increasing scene of glory, opened upon my ravished soul; with a spiritual view of the heavenly hosts surrounding the eternal throne, giving glory to God and the Lamb; with whom, all my ransomed powers seemed to unite, in symphonious strains of divine adoration; feeling nothing but perfect love, peace, joy, and good-will to man pervading all my soul, in a most happy union with God, my all and in all:--every doubt, fear and terror of mind were banished, and heaven opened in my bosom.

In this memorable hour, I have no doubt but God sanctified me to himself, by the power of the Holy Ghost; for, from this time, what had before appeared like insurmountable difficulties, were now made easy, by casting my whole care upon the Lord; and the path of duty was only the path of pleasure. I could pray without ceasing, and rejoice evermore; and my stammering tongue was more than ever loosed, to declare the truth of God, with greater zeal, and affection. At the same time that I received this inestimable blessing, there were many others who were awakened, converted, and made happy in the pardoning love of Christ. The memory of that glorious day will never be erased from my mind.

After I received this divine manifestation of the power of sanctifying grace, I felt a greater desire than ever, to be able to read the scriptures myself, (for as yet I knew nothing of them, but from the reading of others), thinking that by this means I might become more useful. But how to begin to learn this art, at so late a period of life, and prosecute it with success was the difficulty. My children having learned to read and write, and my eldest daughter being now about sixteen years of age, I besought her to undertake her father's instruction; which she did with the utmost cheerfulness, and spared no pains to teach me all she had learned at school; so that in three months from my first beginning, I was able to read the word of God for myself.

But what is most remarkable in this undertaking, was, that she could learn me nothing from the common spelling book; no, not so much as the alphabet; for my mind was so perfectly taken up with the notion of reading the bible, that I could think of nothing else:-- therefore, from this sacred volume she had to instruct me, word by word. The first word of which I learn'd the letters, and how to spell it, was "And;" but, by the blessing of God, I can now read any common book, so as to understand its meaning in general.

The latter part of this year she instructed me how to write, so far as to be able to keep my own accounts; and, though in a broken imperfect manner, to correspond with absent friends, and minute the travels of my own soul in the way to the kingdom, and the dealings of God towards me: a blessing I cannot too highly estimate.

Notwithstanding my illiterature, the Lord was with me in prayer and exhortation; and I trust, added his blessing to my imperfect, but well-meant labors; and while persevering in this way, my mind was impressed with a belief that God required me to preach his gospel in a more direct manner, than my license as an exhorter permitted me to attempt; by which I conceived I might do more good, especially among my African brethren, many of whom I saw rushing head-long into those practices, which, if not repented of, must end in perdition and ruin.

From these views I requested, and was granted the privilege of being heard on trial; when I spake from, "Repent ye therefore, and be converted, that your sins may be blotted out, when the times of refreshing shall come from the presence of the Lord," Acts iv. 19.-- But after hearing me, the brethren in council, concluded I ought not to be licensed as preacher.

Satisfied with this trial, for the present; in the spirit of Christian fortitude, I continued to exhort all sects and denominations of people, as opportunity offered, to repent of their sins; and the Lord assisted me by his grace, and accompanied me with his holy Spirit wherever I went.

About this time, I held an exhorting meeting on Long-Island, which was attended with unusual displays of the divine power. After the people were assembled, and began to pray, numbers of the neighbors came in, and loudly exclaimed against such kind of meetings, as being unnecessary, and prejudicial to society. Upon which I earnestly exhorted all present, who loved God and the souls of men, to unite in one general prayer for a revival of religion in that neighborhood; and God was pleased to hear and answer, by an immediate display of his power, which brought those very declaimers themselves prostrate to the ground, like men who had been shot, beside many others. And scarce could a sinner be in the assembly ten minutes, before he was in the same condition, crying for mercy: and so great was the work, that our meeting continued till ten o'clock next day; in which time, many who came there enemies to God, returned home, praising his name for pardoning mercy and saving grace.

Encouraged by this success attending my labors, I went to New-Lots, and appointed a meeting; and though I had but six hearers, yet perceiving them to be under religious concern, I continued my meetings among them, till God displayed his power, and raised about fifty, to witness his blessing upon my feeble endeavors. All glory to his holy name!

During this little excursion, I had many agreeable and happy prayer meetings; which frequently lasted till midnight; and were attended with peculiar blessings to many who were concerned for the welfare of their souls.

Still impressed with a sense of its being my duty to preach, I made a second application for license. And was permitted to preach another trial sermon; which I did August 22, from "Be not deceived; God is not mocked: for whatsoever a man soweth, that shall he also reap," Gal. vi. 7. but my petition was again rejected.

Soon after this a local preacher called to see me, from whose pious conversation, and account of his own call to preach, I took fresh courage to persevere. We parted in much union, love and fellowship, promising each other never to give up the cause we had espoused, while God continued to witness his divine approbation.

With increasing desires to advance the cause of my adorable Master, I visited the state of New Jersey; and used my utmost endeavors to convince my African brethren in this part, of the necessity of repentance, in order to their salvation. To this work my whole soul and body were devoted; nor did I spare any pains or labor my capacity was capable of, to accomplish so desirable an object: nor yet, did God suffer me to labor and toil in vain, but gave me to witness many wonderful displays of his saving power, in persons of different ages, and even in children.

At one meeting where I was exhorting a numerous body of people, many of the aged of both sexes, fell prostrate under the divine power; acknowledged themselves sinners, and there remained until the Lord converted theirs souls, and gave them the witness of his Spirit: and little children, not more than ten years of age were wrought upon in the same manner; whose cries and prayers for the salvation of their own souls, and the souls of their brethren, for the conviction, and conversion of their ungodly parents, and neighbors; presented a most affecting scene to a feeling mind: at which my own heart glowed with inexpressible joy, and renewed resolution to proceed in obedience to my Master's command; exhorting to repentance all I met with.

The next meeting I attended was at a friend's house, where many assembled to hear. My feelings were much elevated from what I had so recently seen of the manifestations of the grace of God, so that, I spoke with greater confidence in my expectations, believing that more good would result from my labors under his blessing. While speaking, a woman of the neighborhood fell on her knees, and cried aloud for mercy; to the great astonishment of the spectators, and all who were acquainted with her.

Thus I continued exhorting and holding prayer-meetings, and found, that thereby, many of my African brethren, who were strangers to religion before, were now brought to close in with the offers of mercy; among whom I yet hoped to preach the gospel of Jesus Christ, still believing God had called me to this work.

After my return to the city, I made a third application for license, but was told that it was not yet my privilege, and forbid to preach. However, I obtained liberty to preach another trial sermon; which I did from, "Loose him and let him go." John xi. 44. yet the wisdom of God so ordered the consultation of the brethren on the subject, that they determined I should remain as I was, with only my license to exhort. But having previously given them an account of my exercises of mind, and anguish of soul concerning preaching, some of them pitied my condition.

This trial, among others, led me to a more scrutinous enquiry, respecting my own sincerity, and whether I had not been deceived. Under those afflictions and difficulties of mind, I could only vent my anguish and sorrow by crying aloud. I attempted to pray, but could not.

At length it appeared as though something said to my mind, "Remember Johah." I then arose and went to a place where I had appointed to exhort. When I arrived I found the people assembled, and my soul willing to strive to do my duty. In the time of prayer the Lord revived my heart; and at this meeting, manifested himself in the assembly.

I now renewed my resolutions to do all the good I could as an exhorter: accordingly omitted no opportunity in complying with my duty in this respect; warning and beseeching all, whenever opportunity offered, to repent and turn from the evil of their ways, assuring them, from my own experience as well as from scripture, that there is a fullness of mercy in Jesus Christ, for all who will comply with the condition upon which it is offered to sinners: nor did I find sufficient reasons to discourage me from so doing; for my own soul was blessed, and many whom I thus exhorted embraced the Lord Jesus, and became his followers.

It is worthy of remark, however, that those, who from every appearance, set out the fairest for heaven, often turn back again to the world: while many, whose exercises we think but lightly of in their first beginnings, persevere in the way. I noticed an occurrence of this kind, which happened among those where I held a meeting in this city. Two young men, who had spent much of their early days in the vanities of the world; were convinced of sin, and manifested much contrition on the account of it; and both joined society. But the one who shewed the greatest signs of conviction, and could give a rational and affecting account of his situation; soon forsook the cause and people of God: turned again to folly, and is now in the high road to eternal ruin. While the other, who could say little more of himself than, that, he had a desire to serve God, has since experienced religion, and is now a faithful and useful member of society.

What added much to my happiness now was, that I could read the holy scriptures, and converse with my brethren on the important subjects contained therein, which became a source of great delight to my soul under all my trials and conflicts.

About this time, as I was lying in bed, about twelve o'clock at night, and ruminating upon the glories of heaven; all at once my room, which was before entirely dark, became exceeding light, and the appearance of three forms, like doves, presented themselves before my wakeful eyes, who, for some minutes looked me full in the face. A peculiar brightness, or light, surrounding each of them. Conceiving them to be angels, I was terrified with fear; but soon disappearing, and leaving the room dark as before, and me to reflect upon what I had seen, my mind was led to embrace the divine promises; and I considered this vision as an omen of good, and that, in due time, I should reap if I fainted not; for his angels are all ministering spirits, sent forth to minister to them that shall be heirs of salvation.

When upon my several little tours, to different parts of the Island, New Jersey, and elsewhere, nothing so delighted my soul, as to see sinners turning to God, and Christians resolutely warring a good warfare. This, always gave me much encouragement, in pursuing the path of duty, which was pointed out for me by the great head of the church.

And as I generally found it to be attended with a good effect, I frequently declared, not only what I had experienced of the divine favor, but what I had seen of the rich displays of grace and power among others; and by this means encouraging all to trust in, and serve the living God. And I can truly say that many, who before were sitting in darkness, were brought into light and liberty.

But still impressed with the thought, that I was too much circumscribed in my privileges, in December following, I applied again for license to preach: and on the 31st day of the month, preached another trial sermon. My text was, "Let us therefore fear, lest a promise being left us of entering into his rest, any of you should seem to come short of it." Heb. iv. 1. and although the brethren found no fault with the doctrine I preached, nor offered any satisfactory reasons for rejecting my petition, yet they thought I had better remain as I was a while longer. However, I felt no ways concerned, but that, when I had fulfilled the time of probation, allotted me by the great Head of the Church, every objection would be removed from the minds of the brethren, who would then receive me into fellowship as a preacher.

After this, I again visited the people of New Jersey, I had left so happy in the love of God a few months before; and endeavored to encourage them to be faithful to the grace they had already received; by leading their minds to contemplate the glories which await the faithful in the world to come. And used all my efforts, to increase their numbers, by exhorting others to repent, and seek the salvation of their souls. The Lord crowned our meetings with success, and filled us with joy and gladness; while the spirit of love and Christian union, inflamed our hearts.

On my return to the city, I still pursued my usual practice among the brethren, by meeting with them for prayers and exhortation, and found great satisfaction therein. But under my impressions of mind, that God had called me to preach, which I could not resist, I again petitioned to be heard on trial, and obtained the privilege February 14, 1807, when I spoke from, "Behold I send you forth, as sheep, in the midst of wolves: be ye therefore wise as serpents, and harmless as doves." Matth. x. 16:--and the Lord assisted me. But after consultation, the preachers and leaders present, concluded I had better continue to exhort, and let preaching alone for the present: they were not unanimous however in their opinion, yet the majority carried the question against me. On being called before them, to hear their decision, I requested to know if they were dissatisfied with the discourse I had delivered; to which some of them answered in the negative. I then asked if there was anything exceptionable in my character; to which they answered, no. Yet said, they thought it best that I should continue as I was. My mind being somewhat disaffected, at receiving no satisfactory reason, why I was rejected from receiving license to preach; I added; brethren, I have told you the exercises of my mind on the subject; and that I cannot rest without greater liberty than I now enjoy; for I believe God requires me to preach. I was then asked if I had license, whether I could preach any better for it? and what liberty I wanted more than I already had. To which I replied, that I wished to be at liberty to speak from a text, when presented to my mind for that purpose, and I thought God required it of me. But was finally told by one, (from whom I might have expected something more consoling) that it was the devil who was pushing me on to preach. And added, for he wants to raise you up, when he can get a fair shot at you. And his sentiment was seconded by another: at which my mind being extremely agitated with grief and anguish, I cried out; for God's sake, brethren, do not talk thus. And left the place without any to comfort me; my brethren viewing me in the same unfavorable light, that Job's friends did him.

Notwithstanding the great distress and conflicts of mind, occasioned by this last repulse, yet it did not in the least deter me from attending to my duty, but still continued as heretofore, to attend meetings appointed for prayer and exhortation, and constantly found the witness of the divine approbation, accompanying my improvements: for the Lord soon settled my ruffled mind, in a permanent and inviolable peace; which made me satisfied with all his dealings: and willing to suffer any, and everything for his sake.

About this time one of the brethren called on me, and advised me to give up public speaking: for, said he, you will never obtain license to preach. I told him, as long as God would stand by me, I would never give it up. He strove to persuade me, that I was deluded, and said if I persisted, a stop would be put to my exhorting in public; with some other threats of the same nature.

But as I was convinced of his mistake and ignorance in the matter; as also, that God had called me to, and would finally enlarge me in the work; I charged him as in the divine presence, to take care what he did: for if by his opposition, he should become accessary to the loss of but one soul, the consequences to him, must be dreadful. So he left me as he found me, resolved to persevere in the work of God.

As I viewed myself almost friendless, I gave myself much to prayer; and my full heart was expressed in the following words of the poet, which very frequently dwelt upon my mind.

"O that I had a faithful friend,

 "To tell my secrets to:

"On whose advice I might depend,

 "In everything I do.

  "How do I wander up and down;

  "And no one pities me.

"I seem a stranger quite unknown;

"A son of misery.

"None lends an ear to my complaint;

 "Nor minds my cries and tears.

 "None comes to cheer me though I faint,

 "Nor my vast burden bears."

But although my conflicts and trials, from within and without, were so multiplied and great, as at one time to drive me to the very borders of despair; yet the Lord soon revived my soul again, by revealing himself, both in my private, and public devotions; which abundantly encouraged me to persevere, with increasing zeal in the good cause; placing my whole trust and dependence upon God.

And what seemed very much to urge me on in the path of duty, was, reading in the holy scriptures, the threatenings denounced against the disobedient and unfaithful: and fearing, lest the enemy might take advantage of the state of trial I was under, as well as my bodily weakness, I neglected no means, which I thought would be beneficial to my own soul: but particularly fasting and prayer. And what I did myself, I exhorted others to do likewise: considering that they, with myself, must shortly stand before the judgment-seat of Christ, to give an account, for the deeds done in the body.

And I do most sincerely recommend the same practice, to all the followers of Jesus Christ; while they are travelling through this world of snares; especially in seasons of spiritual dullness, or barrenness in religion; for at such times the enemy of souls, is always ready to take the advantage of them; but by fasting, prayer, and faith, his designs may be defeated, and their souls escape, as a bird from the snare of the fowler.

"Lord of the harvest hear
"Thy needy children's cry:
"Answer their faith's effectual pray'r,
"And set them up on high.

"From hell's oppressive pow'r,

"Their struggling souls release:

"And to thy Father's grace restore;

"And to thy perfect peace."

About this time, I had another remarkable dream. In my sleep, a man appeared to me, having under his care a flock of sheep; from which, separating a few, requested I would keep them. But I told him I was no shepherd. However, he went away and left them with me: as he was going, I called after him to know his name: he replied, that it was enough for me to know that he was a shepherd.

This dream encouraged me to hope, that I should find some of the fruit of my labors, in the flock of the great Shepherd of the sheep, at the last day; and inspired me earnestly to pray to God that it might be so.

Feeling it my duty again to go abroad in quest of perishing sinners, and from the exercises of my mind fully believing the time was come, for me to obtain license to preach, I again made application for it; and on the 12th of April preached another trial sermon. My text was, "Cast not away, therefore, your confidence; which hath great recompense of reward." Heb. x. 35. on this occasion, the president elder, and other official characters were present.

We had a comfortable meeting, and my own soul was much strengthened; believing I was doing the will of God; and confidently relying on him for the result, fully resigned my cause to the divine disposal.

The Quarterly Conference was appointed to be held the ensuing evening, when my case must meet a final decision. When the question, whether I should be licensed to preach, was put to vote, a majority of the Conference carried it in the affirmative. But a debate ensued between the president, and presiding elders respecting my preaching abilities. As also whether there was indeed a majority in favor of my being licensed. But by three times counting, it was at last determined that a majority in my favor was no longer disputable. Yet after all, the president elder could not prevail upon the Resident, to give me a license, who objected by saying, he did not believe I was called by the Spirit of God to preach; and if you license him said he to the other, the sin be upon yourself, and you will see before one year, that my words are true.

However the presiding elder had imbibed a more favorable opinion of me, and told him, that, as the Quarterly Conference had voted my license, he should give it to me, for said he, I think better of George than you do, and hope that all his opposers may be disappointed in their predictions about him.

So he gave me license to preach the gospel of Jesus Christ, and encouraged me to go on in the ways of God, and do what I could to bring sinners to repentance and a life of godliness, and to encourage believers, to run for the incorruptible crown of glory.

My mind was now led to a train of reflections, on the dealings of God towards me; in which I discovered so much wisdom and goodness, united with mercy and power, accompanying me through the many changes I had experienced, and effecting my deliverance in times of difficulty and distress; that my mind was overwhelmed with gratitude and love; which I have no language to express.

But this I have learned by experience, that omnipotence itself, is engaged on the side of those who put their trust in him, sincerely obeying the directions of his word and Spirit: and will, sooner or later, though it be through many tribulations, accomplish their deliverance from all their distresses. "O that men would praise the Lord for his goodness, and for his wonderful works to the children of men."

Knowing that, although I had now obtained license to preach, its continuance depended entirely upon my upright conduct and usefulness, as a preacher; and being confident of the divine assistance, I resolved if possible to double my diligence. And that I might the better succeed, as far as possible, to cleanse myself from all filthiness of flesh and spirit; perfecting holiness in the fear of God: and to avoid giving any unnecessary offence; that the gospel might not be blamed through my means.

The better to approve myself, both to God and my brethren, I improved all opportunities while at home, to meet with them at their usual appointments, for prayer and exhortation; and God was with us of a truth; and gave us melting, refreshing times, while I strove in this way to sow the seed in sincerity.

But as it frequently happened, both in the city and country, that even many of the wicked, in the time of religious exercises fell to the earth, under great agitations of mind; I was led to enquire more particularly into the cause of it, from a fear lest some of those I often see fall under my own improvements, might pass through all those extraordinary, external exercises from some other cause than the power of God; and without being either convicted or converted. But upon examination, I could find no better cause to impute it to, than that assigned by St. Paul; who says, "If all prophesy, and there come in one that believeth not, or one unlearned, he is convinced of all, he is judged of all: and thus are the secrets of his heart made manifest; and so, falling down on his face, he will worship God, and report that God is in you of a truth." And thus have I frequently witnessed it to be.

I again visited New-Jersey, and spent one week, in, and about Woodbridge. While preaching here, there was a man in the assembly, who was an avowed enemy to the doctrines taught by the Methodists, and had come to meeting it seems, to speculate upon the people, and look after his wife, who was smitten down by the power of God during the exercises, and his own soul so convicted of sin, that he never rested till he found peace, and is now happy in the Lord.

After my return from Woodbridge, I visited New-Town and Flushing on Long-Island, and the adjacent villages, preaching at every place where I came: and the Lord was among the people in power, and gave us melting, and reviving seasons.

At a place called The Head of the Fly, a little out of Jamaica, I was invited to preach at the house of a coloured man, who was a professed deist. The circumstance much astonished his neighbors: but before I ended my discourse, the word reached his heart with such power, that he roared aloud in the assembly. He has since experienced religion, and is now happy in the love of God. Many others at this meeting, who were before strangers to the power of grace, united with us in prayer to God for mercy: and we parted in much love.

At New Town likewise, I had a good time in preaching to a people, in whose hearts I believe the Lord has effected a gracious work.

The next morning being Sabbath, the white brethren having no preaching that day, I applied to one of the trustees for the privilege of the meeting-house, but was at first refused; being told that I had no authority to preach, or at least that if I had any it was only verbal, and that he had been so informed by D---- C----, a cultured friend from New-York: but on shewing him my license, under the signature of the Presiding Elder, the objection was removed, and the use of the pulpit granted me. We had a gracious manifestation of the presence and power of God; and after preaching I met the classes, of both white, and cultured people, and found them happy in the Lord.

Thus I have found, that, although I have been rejected by some, opposed by others, and suspected by more, that by putting my trust in God, and obeying his will, under all these trials, infinite goodness has caused all events to turn to my account at last; which encourages me, with patience and resignation, to follow Christ, through all the conflicts of the Christianarfare. Besides, I have ever found, that persecution, let it come from what quarter it may, serves only to make me more watchful and prayerful; and when I have endured it awhile longer, I hope, and expect to receive a crown of glory, at the right hand of God.

Having seen much good done this year, in the conversion and sanctification of precious souls, in the several parts where I had employed my time in the labors of the gospel, the period arrived, when I must undergo another examination before my brethren, for the renewal of my license.

At the Quarterly Conference, held in the city of New-York, April 13th, 1808, when my case was called, and some of the African brethren, had offered their animadversions upon my public performances, the Presiding Elder asked if the Conference was not agreed in giving me license at first, and was answered that they were not all agreed.

Elder. Does he preach the gospel?

Brethren. Yes--we believe he does as well as he can.

Elder. And the best can do no more. But have you any objections against his moral character?

Brethren. Not any.

My license was then renewed, and the Elder exhorted the members of the Conference to union among themselves, and to avoid censuring and opposing each other.

The next appointment I attended, which was in this city, tended much to increase my conviction, that I was doing the will of God, as well as lead me to adore the riches of his goodness to sinners.

When I came to the place appointed for me to preach, I found but few assembled. But while waiting for an increase of my congregation, I entertained those present, with an account of my own experience in the things of God; which was so blessed to one of them, that she never rested till she found rest in Jesus, and I trust is now adoring the riches of his grace in a world of glory. Many others were blessed at this meeting, which was evidenced by their loud shouts and earnest prayers. Some of the wicked came to oppose us, but not being able to interrupt our devotions, went away in a rage.

I now visited New-Jersey again, and found in the several towns and villages where I stopped, that religion was in a prosperous way among the cultured, as well as the white people. But the former being my own blood, lay near my heart; so that my chief happiness consisted in seeking to promote their spiritual welfare, by preaching and exhortations among them; and by instructing them in class meetings.

After my return from this little tour, I was appointed to preach in the woods, a little south of Newtown, on Long Island. But before I went to the place where the people were assembling for meeting, the friends told me that a company of ill-disposed people, had collected for the purpose of attacking me on the ground; however I went to the place of appointment, with no other weapons for my defense but the Christian armor, willing to hazard my life thus panoply'd. The congregation was large, and the exercises attended with great power. The people of God were filled with joy and comfort, and many who were hitherto strangers to God, were awakened and converted.

While I was speaking, the company of opposers approached the place of worship, I raised my voice as high as possible, in order that they might hear me; and cried with all my might, "Satan is near the camp;" and exhorted all present, who loved the Lord, to unite in prayer that the designs of the enemy might be defeated. They immediately halted, took their seats upon a fence at a little distance; where they continued for a while, like men confused and ashamed, and then retired, mimicking each other: and left us to God and ourselves, to proceed in our devotions without disturbance. The wrath of man shall praise the Lord, and the remainder will he restrain.

Soon after this I returned to New-Jersey, which I had but recently left, in order to help forward the good work among my African brethren there, on this visit, much of my time was taken up in Brunswick, Shrewsbury, Middletown and Woodbridge; where I had good times, and the Lord attended my labors with much success.

After my return, I prepared for a journey to the south, with a view of visiting my native land, to see my parents, and how it fared with those of my own color, who I left in a state of slavery a number of years before; in hopes of being beneficial to their souls; for my heart had often felt the keenest anguish for them.

With these views, I set off towards the last of this year, and arriving at Trenton, New-Jersey, I tarried two days, and preached twice from the following words, "Seek ye the Lord, while he may be found, call ye upon him while he is near." Isaiah lv. 6. and, "For ye were sometimes darkness, but now are ye light in the Lord; walk as children of the light." Eph. v. 8.

My soul was much refreshed among the people in this place, who appeared united in the sanctified bonds of the purest friendship; and the work of God successfully advancing among them.

My next stage was the city of Philadelphia: where I spent two weeks. Here I found my cultured brethren much alive to God, and the interest of the Redeemer's kingdom. I preached in their churches, and was abundantly comforted.

From thence I went to Wilmington; state of Delaware; where I spent a week in visiting and preaching among my African brethren, who appeared to enjoy all the sweets of religion, and was much delighted with hearing them relate their experience in the things of God, and tell of his grace and goodness towards them, and leaving them engaged for heaven I set off for Baltimore.

Arriving there, I spent about two weeks in visiting the brethren; and was agreeably disappointed in finding many with whom I had been acquainted when a slave in Virginia; who were then in the broad road to misery: but had now become the children of the living God. At least, bore every appearance of being such; having become sober, honest and industrious, as well as professors of the religion of Jesus Christ: so that all appeared to be happy around them. During my stay among them, I preached frequently, and particularly urged upon the brethren as a duty, the necessity of using every means in their power, both by prayer, instruction and exhortation, to bring as many of their acquaintance as possible, who were yet in their sins, to the knowledge of the truth, as it is in Jesus Christ. I then preached a farewell discourse from, "The Lord direct your hearts, into the love of God, and into the patient waiting for Christ." 2 Thess. iii. 5. I took my leave of them, commending them to God and the word of his grace, and pursued my journey to Somerset county.

But, when I reached this place, not finding as I expected, my aged parents, who had obtained their freedom, and removed to a great distance from this; nor more than half a dozen persons I had formerly been acquainted with, I spent but a short time among them; during which, I preached but twice, took my leave of them, and set out for home.

On my return, I revisited the brethren at Wilmington, with whom I tarried several days, which I spent in visiting, prayers, exhortation and preaching, and the Lord accompanied my labors with divine power, so that, at several of our meetings, much good was done in the name of the Lord Jesus.

From Wilmington, I came to Philadelphia; where I spent five days in the same exercises; and then left the followers of the Redeemer, in joyful hope of meeting them in heaven, if no more upon the earth.

I next stopped at Cranberry, state of New Jersey; where I made a short stay; visited, and preached with the brethren, and parted from them in much love and friendship.

On my arrival at New York, I found my family in good health: and the work of God prospering among my African brethren, in like manner, as I had found it in the south.

After the rest and refreshment necessary from so long a journey, I again visited the brethren upon Long Island, where I renewed my labors with much success. The people

here, who had formerly been very unstable;
from the many reproofs they had received,
were now willing to unite with the children of
God.

After preaching at a place called Little
Neck, from, "How shall we escape if we
neglect so great salvation." Heb. ii. 3. a person
of a different sentiment from the Methodists,
came to me, and said, you have given us all to
the devil (meaning his own denomination,) I
told him that I gave no Christian of any
denomination to the devil; but taught that the
wicked would be damned if they did not
repent, and endeavored to convince him of the
truth of what I had preached. After some time
he became pacified, and he, with others of his
own persuasion, invited me to preach among
them at a place several miles distant from this,

for which I gave them an appointment, and two weeks after preached to them from, "The last day, that great day of the feast, Jesus stood and cried, saying, if any man thirst, let him come unto me and drink." John vii. 37. the meeting was solemn and conducted with great order. The congregation was principally composed, of Africans and Indians. The Lord was present in power, and began a glorious revival of religion among this people, with whom I have since enjoyed many happy seasons of Christian intercourse and fellowship.

In the beginning of 1809, I made a little excursion to the northward of York Island, and spent about three weeks at Singsing, Westchester, and the adjacent villages; and found that many of the brethren in those parts, were much engaged with God, and determined, through grace to press towards the mark, for the prize of their high calling, in Christ Jesus. I enjoyed much satisfaction, in preaching, and other religious exercises among them, being accompanied with the refreshing manifestations of the divine power and presence.

After my return, I spent some time in attending the little meetings about the city, where God was carrying on his work, and gathering converts into the church. After which I went again to Long Island, and found the cause of God advancing among the people, and sinners daily seeking shelter in the ark of safety, and uniting themselves with the followers of the Lord Jesus. At Jerusalem while preaching from, "Cry aloud, spare not, lift up your voice like a trumpet, and shew my people their transgressions, and the house of Jacob their sins." the Lord attended his word with power, one woman was converted, and I had reason to believe much good was done. At this place and the neighboring villages, I continued preaching and exhorting on all suitable occasions until the latter part of this year, and in the meantime assisted my Christian brethren in building an house for the Lord at Jerusalem.

On my return home, I was informed by my family that sister Mary Henery had been sick for some considerable time, and had repeatedly sent for me during my absence, to visit her. I went immediately to her master's house (for she was a slave) to see her, and found her extremely weak, and exercised with great bodily pain. On my entering her room she cried out, "Glory to God, brother, have you come?" Yes, said I, sister, for Christ's sake I have come.

I then inquired the state of her soul; to which she replied; I am as happy as I can be in the body. After which she sunk into a state of perfect insensibility to every outward object, and to all appearance lay entirely lifeless for some time. But after so far recovering as to be able to speak, she broke out in loud shouts of praise to God, and said, that while she was in that state she saw the gates of heaven opened, and a beautiful company of shining personages arrayed in white robes. And observed that she had often thought how delightful the singing was in the Methodist church, but that was incomparable with the singing of these angels in glory; with whom she expected shortly to join, and stated the moment her soul would leave the body for that purpose.

I asked if I should pray with her, she said, "yes, brother, pray that my faith fail not." While I was engaged in this exercise, she broke out aloud in prayer herself, for the welfare of her mistress and young master (his father being dead,) and earnestly besought the Lord to convert his soul, and to extend the same blessing to all mankind. The fervency of her prayer and the energy of the language with which it was clothed, so affected all present, that they were scarce able to stand.

I attended her on the day of her death, being October 28, 1809; three days after my first visit; and found her perfectly sensible, and resigned to the will of God. She said she was glad to see me, as she

had something particular to say to her mother and me.

After entreating her aged mother in the most affectionate manner, not to weep on her account, as she was fully assured to arriving shortly at the place of eternal rest, she proceeded to give some advice respecting her own funeral preparations and solemnities, earnestly requesting that her corps might be dressed in a plain white shroud, without a ruffle, or any other ornament; and especially, that there might be no kind of spirituous liquor drank at her funeral, adding, that she had observed the practice of drinking, at a number of funerals which she had attended, and spoke of it in the highest terms of disapprobation, as being both improper and indecent.

Between eleven and twelve o'clock the following evening, she requested her mother to call the family together into her room. When they were come, she told them, that her soul, which was bound for heaven, would shortly quit the mortal body: but said she, "I shall give you the signal for my departure by shouting, being fully assured of dying triumphant in the faith."

Her father being present, she earnestly exhorted him to forsake the evil of his ways and turn to God, that he might meet her in a world of glory, to which she was now going. Her words much affected him, having reached his heart with convincing power; and from that moment he set out to seek the Lord, and is now a zealous member of Christ's Church, of which her mother was previously a pious member.

As she drew near the moment she had said she should expire, she asked her mother (who was quite feeble) if she would shout with the rest present, when she gave the word: who, although in great anguish of soul, on account of the prospect of parting with so excellent a child, told her she would, but not expecting the time was so near. But she soon repeated her request, and said, "Mother, help me all you can to praise God; I know you are weak, but come around my bed and get ready, for the chariot is coming--are you all ready? Are you all ready? Now! now! Here it comes.

Glory! Glory! Glory! Shout! Shout! Mother, are you shouting? *

* JANE was her fellow-servant.

Jane, are you shouting? Are you all shouting? And thus continued till she expired, which was at the very moment she had before said she should die.

Thus happy and triumphant died our dear young sister, the daughter of George and Sarah Henery, in the twentieth year of her age; and as she died, so she had lived after her conversion to God, which was but about two years before her death: during which time she had walked exemplary in all the ways of God, both towards her Redeemer, and her fellow-creatures; and to say the least of her that justice demands, she was modest, decent, sober and diligent; in short, she possessed all the embellishments of the most chaste female character, to a degree seldom equaled, especially by those in a state of slavery. However, her master and mistress (Mr. and Mrs. Post,) had always treated her with much indulgence and great kindness, both in sickness and health; and when she died, the old lady and her son, as well as all present, were much affected with the scene.

She had experienced sanctification at the Croton Camp-Meeting, the year before her death; and the last time she met in class, she told one of the sisters, that she should meet with her no more in those religious exercises on earth; being fully persuaded that God, who had prepared her for a better world, was about to take her to himself.

To her case, the language of the poet is truly applicable.

"Happy soul, thy days are ended:
"All thy mourning days below.
"Go, by angel guards attended;
"To the sight of Jesus go.

"Waiting to receive thy spirit:
"Lo, the Savior stands above:
"Shews the purchase of his merit;
"Reaches out the crown of love.

"Struggle through thy latest passion:

"To thy dear Redeemer's breast:

"To his uttermost salvation;

"To his everlasting rest.

"For the joy he sets before thee;

"Bear a momentary pain.

"Die to live a life of glory.

"Suffer, with thy Lord to reign."

I cannot but here remark, that while we
see the souls of the righteous leaving the
world, with loud shouts of joy and praise to
God; that it is not to be wondered at, that
individuals or whole assemblies of the people
of God, in life and health, being filled with the
joys of that hope which is full of immortality,
should sometimes "Clap their hands, and
shout unto God with the voice of triumph," as

saith the Psalmist; or in correspondence with the sentiments of Isaiah, "should sing and shout because the holy one of Israel is great in the midst of them. For that the upright in heart" should "shout for joy," while heavenly glory beams upon their ravished souls, can be nothing astonishing to the sincere Christian, who has "felt the powers of that world to come;" where all the glorified host of God's elect continually cry with voices louder than many waters, and mighty thunders; glory "to him that has washed us from our sins in his own blood, and made us kings and priests unto God and the Father; to whom be glory for ever and ever."

As God had made me instrumental in the awakening and conversion of this young sister, and being present at her death, her parents requested me to preach her funeral sermon; the substance of which, at their desire, I shall here insert; with an Elegy, composed on the death of their daughter. The defects of which, candor will find an easy apology for, considering the opportunities I have had to improve my mind in erudition.

THE SUBSTANCE OF A SERMON, PREACHED ON THE FUNERAL OCCASION OF MARY HENERY.

From "Strive to enter in at the strait gate, for many I say unto you shall seek to enter in, and shall not be able." Luke xiii. 34.

THE occasion on which we are assembled this day, is truly solemn, interesting and alarming; being met together to pay our last respects to the remains of our departed sister, who but recently filled her usual seat in this house; and rejoiced, on all religious occasions, to unite with you, my brethren, in chanting the songs of Zion, with an heart filled with the love of Christ, and exulting in the joys of his salvation.

But she is now no more: and though called to lament the loss of so worthy a member of the Church of Christ; yet we do not mourn as those without hope, for, "Them that sleep in Jesus, God will bring with him," at the last day; and our Savior says, he "came to seek and to save that which was lost:" and in the chapter of which our test is a part, he intimates, that the chief of sinners may be saved who will repent; by preaching the doctrine of repentance, from the circumstance of the Gallaleans, whose blood Pilate mingled with their sacrifices; and that without repentance, none can be saved. But this blessing our departed sister had no doubt attained, with whom we hope to join in strains of immortal praise hereafter, when our bodies shall have endured the original sentence denounced against us for sin, "Dust thou art, and unto dust shalt thou return." For like her, through Jesus Christ we may obtain victory over death, hell and the grave, by complying with the terms of our text, which says, "Strive to enter in at the strait gate, for many I say unto you, shall seek to enter in, and shall not be able."

From which I shall take the liberty briefly to shew,

First, What we are to understand by the strait gate, and how we are to enter in thereat.

Secondly, Why it is called strait. And,

Thirdly, Who they are that shall seek to enter in, and shall not be able. And,

I. I am to shew what we are to understand by the strait gate, and how we are to enter in thereat. By the strait gate we are undoubtedly to understand, Jesus Christ himself, who has said, "I am the way, and the truth, and the life; no man cometh unto the Father but by me." And again: "Strait is the gate and narrow is the way that leadeth to life, and few there be that find it." "I am," says he, "the door, by me if any man enter in he shall be saved, and go in and out and find pasture."

Christ then being "the strait gate," and his doctrines the narrow way, and himself the only door of admission to the favor of God, and salvation; the scripture directs us how we are to enter in thereat, that is, by repentance, and faith in the merit of the atonement he has made for sinners, by the once offering of himself to God without spot.

By faith, then, we are to enter in at this gate: for although it is said, "Strive to enter in at the strait gate," yet we are to place no dependence upon our labors or strivings; for we can do nothing effectual in our own salvation, only as far as we are assisted by the all-sufficient grace of God; for it is written, "By grace are ye saved, through faith, and that not of yourselves, it is the gift of God."

Yet although our strivings alone cannot prove effectual to our salvation, in this way, however, we must come to Christ, and receive him into our hearts. Therefore, "Strive to enter in at the strait gate, for many I say unto you shall seek to enter in, and shall not be able." But,

II. Why is this gate called strait? I answer: from the example Christ has left us, that we should follow his steps, which is directly contrary to the corruptions of our own natures; and because repentance and faith, by which we must enter in thereat, are crossing, humbling and self-renouncing; in the attainment of which, the soul is brought into great inward straits of fear, terror and difficulty, but is always accompanied with hope of mercy, and followed with a revelation of Jesus Christ, as the all-sufficient Savior, to such as commit the care of their souls to him, trusting in his mercy alone for pardon and eternal salvation; and if adhered to, will lead to that eternal rest of glory, which our departed sister this day enjoys, in the presence of God and the Lamb. Therefore, "Strive to enter in at the strait gate, for many I say unto you shall seek to enter in, and shall not be able."

I am 3dly, and lastly to shew, who they are that shall seek to enter in, and shall not be able.

There is no impediment to our entering in at the strait gate, but what originates in ourselves; for Christ has said, "He that cometh unto me, I will in no wise cast out:" and assigns it as the only reason why men are not saved, that they will not come unto him, that they might have life. And they do not come to Christ, because their hearts are opposed to his government, and his ways too crossing to their carnal inclinations.

But says the text, "Many shall seek to enter in, and shall not be able:" either because they do not seek aright, or in good earnest, by forsaking all their sins, resisting evil of every kind and degree; and by an agonizing, wrestling spirit, which refuses to be comforted, till Christ is formed in the heart the hope of glory.

Or lastly, because they seek too late; which is the reason Christ assigns in the words immediately following the text, "Strive to enter in at the strait gate, for many I say unto you shall seek to enter in, and shall not be able;" for, "When once the master of the house is risen up, and hath shut to the door, and ye begin to stand without, and to knock at the door, saying, Lord, Lord, open unto us; and he shall answer and say unto you, I know you not whence ye are, depart from me all ye workers of iniquity." How sad the disappointment, to seek for mercy too late to find it; even at the hand of him, who now says,

"Behold, I stand at the door and knock; if any man hear my voice, and will open the door, I will come in to him, and will sup with him, and he with me.

IMPROVEMENT.

Whoever would go to heaven then, must repent, and believe in Jesus Christ, who is the only door of salvation, the way, the truth, and the life; and as our Lord said to Nichodemus, must be born again, or they cannot see the kingdom of God: for except renewed by the grace of God, in the very nature of things, no man can be happy; for the very nature of sin prevents the enjoyment of God, the only source and fountain of all happiness; so that, whoever dies without being renewed, must meet the just reward of their ungodliness, in the awful day of judgment, when the secrets of all hearts shall be revealed.

As this change of heart is called entering in at the strait gate, because it implies self-denial, mortification, self-renunciation, conviction and contrition for sin; and as all this is directly contrary to the dispositions of corrupt nature, it requires great and constant exertions, and mighty struggles of soul, under the influences of divine grace, to attain the blessing. For let none vainly imagine, that barely wiping their mouth will excuse them from damnation, or answer as a substitute for inward and outward holiness, in the great day of the wrath of God Almighty, when he shall come to judge the world in righteousness: therefore, "Seek ye the Lord while he may be found, call ye upon him while he is near: let the wicked forsake his way, and the unrighteous man his thoughts, and let him turn unto the Lord, who will have mercy upon him, and to our God, for he will abundantly pardon.

And in this great and important work there is no time for delay; for life, the utmost extent of the day of grace, is uncertain; which is not only proved by the common occurrences of every day, but particularly by the instance of mortality which has occasioned our convention at this time; which speaks to you in the most pathetic language: "Be ye also ready, for in such an hour as ye think not the Son of man cometh;" and when once "the master of the house is risen up, and shut to the door, and ye begin to stand without, and to knock, saying, Lord, Lord, open unto us;" you will only be answered with, "depart from me all ye that work iniquity:" therefore now return unto the Lord from whom you have departed, by sincere repentance, that your souls may live. Secure a supply of the oil of grace, trim your lamps, and prepare to meet the bridegroom at his coming, that ye may enter in to the marriage supper of the Lamb, before the door of mercy is forever shut.

I see before me a large number of mourners, whose showering tears bespeak the anguish of heart excited by the death of her, whose relies we have so recently followed to the house appointed for all the living. But hush the heaving sigh, and dry the briny tear, for your deceased relative, and our much-loved Christian sister, has, no doubt, found a safe passage through the strait and narrow gate to the blissful regions of eternal day; where she now joins the Church triumphant, around the dazzling throne of God, in songs of praise and shouts of victory.

And while you, with the rest of this congregation, have the offers of mercy yet held out to you in the name of Jesus Christ, who stands knocking at the door of your hearts for entrance; embrace it, and bid him welcome, that you may be prepared when death shall call you hence, to join the jubilant throng with our departed sister, and chant the wonders of redeeming grace forever.

But to you, especially, who are in the bloom of youth, this instance of mortality calls aloud to prepare for death; remember your all is at stake; death is at your door, and will shortly summon you to appear at the bar of God, who will assuredly bring you into judgment for living after the desires of your own wicked hearts. Reflect then for a moment, how awful it will be to die in your sins, strangers to God, and meet the awful Judge of quick and dead, to hear the sentence pronounced upon your guilty souls, "Depart ye cursed into everlasting fire, prepared for the devil and his angels." To avert this dreadful doom delay no longer; but now, even now, embrace the offers of mercy tendered to you by the gospel of Jesus Christ, and experience his great salvation.

And finally, brethren, let us all consider our ways, turn to the Lord, and strive to enter in at the strait gate, that we may not be found among the number of those, who by seeking too late, shall not be able to enter in; that when we are called to lie upon our death bed, we may have the same ravishing views of heaven, our departed sister had two days before her death, who said, she "saw heaven opened, and heard the saints in glory sing:" and like her, leave the world, crying glory! glory! glory! even so, Lord Jesus. Amen! and Amen!

I here subjoin the following elegy, composed on the death of our departed sister in Christ.How wondrous are thy ways, Almighty God! Deep are they councils; and severe thy rod! Thy chastening hand, what mortal man can stay? Or who can turn thy tenderness away?

Our friend is gone, but let us not repine:
The gem was ravished by the hand divine.
Call'd to adorn the dear Redeemer's crown,
And add new honors to Immanuel's throne.

Her virtue lives; and ever live it must;

Although her flesh lies slumbering in the

dust.

Wipe off the tear, suppress the swelling

sigh;

For she that lives in Christ can never die.

Grieve not, ye parents, give your sighing

o'er:

The deep felt cause will soon be felt no

more.

Your daughter lives in pleasures ever

new,

On Zion's hill, where she looks

out for you.

I shall now present the reader with the striking, but awful contrast with what I have just related, and which took place soon after. A very prophane (cultured) man, who was a great enemy to religion, living but a little distance from me, on his being taken sick, his wife, who was a serious woman, (but not allowed by her husband to attend religious meetings) sent for me to come and see him. I accordingly went, and continued to visit him every day while he lived; but found him, through his whole sickness, the most hardened obstinate sinner I ever met with. I conversed, prayed with, and exhorted him to no effect; for the most I could induce him to say of himself was, that he hoped or expected to recover. But the eighth day of his sickness, being Sabbath, and the day on which he died,

I was sent for in the morning to go and see him. On coming to the house, I was informed by his wife, that, apprehending himself struck with death, he had that morning attempted to run away, asserting that he was flying from death, which he saw after him; but was apprehended and brought back by the neighbors. Upon hearing this, I concluded he was insane; but was soon convinced otherwise, and that his conduct was the effect of dread and terror: for on every other subject he appeared perfectly rational. I conversed with him about the sad condition his soul was in, and inquired of him the reason why he attempted to run away.--He replied, that death was after him. I told him that it was in vain to attempt to make his escape from death; but ought rather to seek a preparation for it. He observed, that in this respect it was a gone case with him: for, said he, "I am a damned wretch," and broke out in the most horrid oaths. After the morning service I visited him again, being accompanied by brother A. T. a local preacher, who asked him some questions concerning his condition; to which he answered, that it was a gone case with him, and began to curse and swear so horribly, that neither of us could find it in our hearts to pray with him. I called again, as did many others, towards evening, to see this wonder of depravity, and found him in the same frame of mind as before. He said the devils had come for him, and that he could see them all about the room. I asked him why he went on in the manner he did: he declared that he could not help it. I went to see him for the last time between ten and eleven o'clock at night, and left him about half an hour before his death belching out the most impious oaths and curses, which I was told he continued to do till death put a stop to it. Thus, living without the fear of God, he died in a state of mad despair, where we leave him, with the reader to reflect upon the awful contrast between such a death, and that of the young woman before mentioned; not doubting but his good sense will teach him which to prefer as his own. But withal remember, that if you would die the death of the righteous, in preference to that of the wicked, you must live their life also.

Before I close this little narrative, I will offer a few thoughts on the subject of true happiness, being the result of my own experience and observation, as well as suggested by the doctrines of the gospel of Jesus Christ.

Happiness is the grand object of the pursuit of every man. But alas! how many fail of its attainment, by seeking for it where it is not to be found.

But what is happiness? it may be asked, and where, and how is it to be obtained? To these inquiries none but the real Christian, who lives in the light of the sanctuary, can give a decided and satisfactory answer.

God is the only source of true happiness;--and happiness therefore consists in the enjoyment of God only; and is in no other way to be obtained but by such a faith in Jesus Christ, as unites the soul to him, and possesses it of that "Righteousness, peace, and joy in the Holy Ghost," which the apostle Paul denominates the "Kingdom of God;" and is the well-spring of that joy and rejoicing, which he elsewhere recommends to the truly pious, by saying, "Rejoice in the Lord always, and again I say rejoice."

The Divine perfections, attributes, and government, are a continual source of happiness and joy to the real Christian; for being united to God, he not only discovers their beauty and harmony, but rests in the fullest assurance, that they are all engaged to make him blessed, while he enjoys the witness of the amazing mercy of God, in the free pardon of all his sins.

He rejoices in the wisdom of God, as ordering all events, and as being engaged for his direction, in whatever station or condition of life, Divine Providence may have placed him, being fully persuaded that God will neither do, nor suffer to be done, what he would not do, or suffer to be done himself, could he but see the end of all things as perfectly as God does:--therefore he is contented and happy under all his dealings, knowing that adversity, pain and sickness, shall no less turn to his advantage, under the direction of infinite wisdom and goodness, than prosperity, case, health and wealth; for whom the Lord loveth he chasteneth, and scourgeth every son whom he receiveth: and will make all things work together for good to them that love him.

The power and omnipresence of God, are equally a source of the Christian's joy, for being everywhere at the same time, and able to accomplish all his purposes, can, not only purify his heart from sin, but give him victory over all his temporal and spiritual enemies, and afford support under every trial and burden.

So that the soul who trusts in the Lord Jesus, who has himself, conquered all his enemies, rejoices in full assurance of being made more than conqueror, through Christ who has loved him. For he is a friend that sticketh closer than a brother.

Our earthly friends may be absent when we want them most, and if present, would not in all cases know how to help us, if they would;

nor have they it in their power in all cases to do it, and even the best of them may prove treacherous to our interest, and ruin us forever. But not so with our heavenly friend, who is infinitely wise, powerful, and good, whose veracity is pledged, that he will never leave nor forsake them who put their trust in him. Therefore, the true Christian must be happy.

The holy scriptures, which reveal the divine character and government, our duty to God and one another; and especially, as they assure the righteous of a glorious immortality, are an inexhaustible source of joy and rejoicing to the Christian, while every promise teems with the honey of everlasting love, and glares with the full blaze of future glory, upon the dazzled eyes of him who reads them by faith, as his own through grace.

In allusion to which, St. Austin says, "the word of God is like the starry heavens in a clear night:" "if," says he "you cast your eyes upon a given part of it, some stars immediately discover themselves to your view; but the more attention you give, the more stars will be breaking forth to the sight:" and so it is with the sacred scriptures, ever new, and ever unfolding new beauties, and increasing glories, to all the persevering followers of the Lord Jesus.

The works of creation, which the mere philosopher views only as a series of natural causes and effects, unfold to the ravished sight of faith, the eternal power and God-head, beaming its own divine effulgence from every branch of the natural world; and the loving heart feels that he who made the stars is my Father and my God, under whose control are all the elements; these are the works of my great Redeemer, my Savior, and my Friend, which all obey his sovereign will, and declare his matchless glory; from whose gracious hand, the most trifling benefit is received with the highest sensations of gratitude, and thus becomes a lasting blessing; while the greatest favors heaven can bestow upon the impenitent, through their un-thankfulness, become but lasting curses, and serve to enhance their condemnation.

Indeed, nothing on earth can equal the Christian's happiness, and nothing else deserves that endearing name For who can be so happy as he who knows his sins are all forgiven, that God is his reconciled Father and Friend; that he is entitled, through the merit of Jesus Christ, to the protection of the Almighty, and coheirship with his Son hereafter; for the security of which, the veracity of God himself is pledged, all whose promises in Christ Jesus are yea and amen. Who so happy as they that have an hope full of immortality beyond the grave, and are assured that all things shall work together for their good; so that their very sufferings shall only work out for them, a far more exceeding and eternal weight of glory. It was these things, which the apostle John wrote to his brethren, that their joy might be full. It is by entering deep into the spirit of these things, that the joy of Christ is fulfilled in the believer; and to be the helpers of their joys, has Jesus Christ sent his ministers with this commission, "Comfort ye, comfort ye my people, saith your God;" and the more of this comfort the Christian enjoys, with the greater contempt does he look down upon all earthly pleasure, and crucifies himself the more to the world.

And as he partakes of the nature, as well as the enjoyment of God, it is his chief delight to diffuse happiness among his fellow-creatures, as far as is in his power, which only increases his joy, by the necessary happiness which arises from doing good to others, and making them happy; which returns to God in constant strains of adoration from every happy soul. May the God of grace and love, make the reader thus unspeakably happy in himself, and his service, and at last, bring both you and me to enjoy a state of consummate happiness, in the full enjoyment of his glory, in the world to come.

FINIS.

www.ingramcontent.com/pod-product-compliance
Lightning Source LLC
Chambersburg PA
CBHW051430090426
42737CB00014B/2899